P. PASQUALE MAGRO OFM Conv.

ASSISI

History Art Spirituality

CASA EDITRICE FRANCESCANA - 06082 ASSISI - FRATI MINORI CONVENTUALI

PRINTED IN ITALY: UMBRIAGRAF TERNI

Visions of Franciscan Assisi

Asisium, Ascesi, Assisi: the very evolution of the city's name is a sign to the visitor that here may be found a rich harvest of admirable masterpieces, the relics of many past civilizations. For native Umbrians, Etruscans, Romans, Byzantines and Lombards have all left indelible footprints which, despite human negligence, have survived to this day claiming respect and wonder.

The topographical shape of the city, made bright and unmistakable by the distinguished focalpoint of the Basilica containing the Tomb of St. Francis and the Sacro Convento, the somber and clear lines of the ascending urban mass built from the local pink and white stone, the figures in the fading multicolored tints of the pictorial texts in the old churches, are already a silent language magnificently speaking the thousand historical stories that have matured the present image of this city resting at the foot of Mount Subasio.

It was Francis of Assisi (1182-1226) with his human and Christian experience, suspended between legend and history, who determined the present aspect of the city, enviable for its mystery and spiritual atmosphere.

The visions of Assisi presented in this book through the language of photographic art, do not aim only at bringing back to life the actors and events that have left their mark upon the remote past of this timeless city, but aim also at spurring all who respond to its charm, to set out in search of ever more alluring and true endeavors through which they can find, in freedom and joy of spirit, their own authentic and fulfilled humanity.

**"ASSISI,
beloved city of God"**
(Legend of St. Clare)

The City-Shrine

The privileged places which have known the physical presence of Saint Francis are called "shrines" or "holy places" since in each of them Francis has left traces of his holiness: *"Capable of every grace, a chosen vessel of virtue, he poured out his gifts on all sides"* (**Thomas of Celano**).

No shrine considered in itself can boast exclusively of radiating the great soul of the Saint, but only the ensemble of Franciscan shrines can reveal to visitors and pilgrims the royal, prophetical and priestly traits of this great Christian of Assisi. Burning with zeal for God, humanity, and nature, he enveloped them in the revitalizing fragrance still evident in our day.

At **San Damiano,** Francis brought to life his desire for moral conversion and his tormenting search for the "one thing necessary" after his dramatic departure from the old familiar world.

At the **Portiuncola** he overflowed with apostolic zeal, and wished to share with all Christians his own joyful personal experience of being pardoned by God, by instituting the Portiuncola Indulgence.

In the privation of the **Rivotorto** huts, he lived to the full his desire for conversion and apostolic mission in fraternity and minority with his first followers.

At the **Carceri,** he experienced an abundant and profound awareness of union with the Eternal Spouse.

On the **Square** and **streets** he generously spread the "peace and goodness" of God and did not fail to act as a peacemaker whenever possible. In the **free and open countryside** he was enlivened by the desire to be with the Infinite and the whole cosmos.

In the many **Churches of the city,** his burning words enlightened his hearers and urged them all to cultivate an ardent love for God, for their oppressed brothers and sisters, and for the forgotten universe of God's creatures, both animate and inanimate.

Overflowing with Christian authenticity, having lived for forty-four years, Francis entered into eternity with abundant joy, only to return like transcendent dew, to inspire centuries of Christian civilization, spirituality, and art.

Of this abundant Franciscan grace, the Basilica of Assisi, a dream from the heart of Gregory IX and of the daring mind of Brother Elias, intending to guard in its depths the "broken vessel" of the body of the Saint, is a summary, symbol, and reality expressed most expressively in the language of art.

The gothic, sober, but festive themes of the Upper Church as well as the Romanesque, tense and thoughtful style of the Lower Basilica, the colorful flood of light which flows wonderously from the stained glass windows of both Churches, are an invitation to all visitors to descend to the rough underground Crypt to whisper a prayer before the tomb of St. Francis' "Brother body", the Franciscan shrine *par excellence*.

The Basilica of St. Francis

Historical Development and Cultural Significance

'For the unquestionable reverence he had toward the holy Father Francis, (blessed Giles) insisted that on his tomb an eminent church should be built so that the idea of his outstanding holiness could impress itself upon the minds of the people"
(Ubertino da Casale)

The architectural triptych

As in the case of so many famous shrines, the history of the Basilica of St. Francis in Assisi is rooted in legend.

The location of the church, the "hill of hell", had formerly been a burial place for wrong-doers of all kinds, especially enemies of the city, but was completely transformed in character by Gregory IX, who renamed it the "Hill of Paradise". Before his death, Francis told his closest companions that he longed to be buried within sight of the town where he had been born, but wished that his body might rest among these wrong-doers and outcasts, and in imitation of Christ who died among thieves and was buried outside of Jerusalem. (St. Bonaventure, Major Life, VI, 2).

We read in codex 8, from the XIV Century, in the Chiesa Nuova in Assisi: *"When Blessed Father Francis was nearing death, his companions asked him: 'Father, where do you want to be buried?' and he answered: 'Where the gallows of wrong-does are.' What in fact happened is above the spot where he was buried, stands the main altar of the Basilica, where there had been a place of justice'."*

On March 29, 1228, Brother Elias Bombarone received, in the name of the Holy Father, this hillside to the west of the city where the Church was to be built. The gift was made by Simone Pucciariello, a devout citizen of Assisi. Francis was canonized on July 16, 1228, and on the following day, Gregory IX laid the foundation stone of the Church. *"It seems right and fitting to us,"* wrote the Pope, *"that in reverence towards the same Father, a Church should be erected wherein to lay his mortal remains" (Bull* **Recolentes,** *1228).* Work on the new Basilica progressed rapidly as the Brother responsible for its direction gave himself fully to the task, and on May 25, 1230, the body of Francis was laid to rest in what was to be its final burial place.

Nine years later the main structure had been completed; this included the bell tower containing the first bell named "Italia" cast by Bartolomeo of Pisa and dedicated by Brother Elias to Gregory IX and Frederick II. It was Innocent IV, who in 1253 consecrated the great Basilica, which now consisted of two superimposed churches crowning **St. Francis' Tomb.** The Lower Church in Lombard Romanesque style, with a single central nave in the form of the latin cross, acted as the crypt. Its rough low structures supported what came to be known as the Upper Church, stylistically the first example of Italian Gothic architecture. Towards the end of the XIII Century, side chapels, all gothic in style, were added to the Lower Church.

In 1818, St. Francis' remains were exhumed for the first time and a crypt, in neo-classical style, was dug from solid rock. Alterations were made in 1932 by Ugo Tarchi, with the result that the crypt's present architectural structure is neo-romanesque.

At the present time, the architectural triptych rises like a hymn of praise in perfect harmony of fabric and color, inspired by the perfect joy and freedom of spirit of "The Herald of the Great King", Francis of Assisi. The historian, Adolfo Venturi, has described the Basilica as *"the most beautiful house of prayer of which this earth can boast".*

The pictorial text

The Basilica of Assisi claims to house "the most extraordinary composition of pictorial art of the Italian middle ages" (F. Santi). The friars and the local population, untouched by any leaning toward the iconoclastic spirit characteristic of the times of spiritual reform, gave free vent to their love of color in decorating the church. But there is no doubt that the originality of the architecture was what permitted such a display of pictorial splendor. J. von Schlosser writes: *"The first memorable monument constructed in Italian-gothic style, the Church of St. Francis, built in Assisi only a few years after the death of the Saint, already reveals a decidedly Italian characteristic, matching in its perfect balance, the sound common sense of the Italian people. In this Church, the walls have been destined from the beginning to be decorated with frescoes and these play a much more important role than the walls of Gothic Churches in Northern Europe."*

The first artist called by Brother Elias to inaugurate the Assisi artistic period was Giovanni Capitini from Pisa. In 1236 he hoisted the huge "Franciscan Crucifix" onto the iconostasis of the Upper Church upon which the Minister General appears in prayful attitude at the foot of the "Christus Patiens". Unfortunately, the cross was lost in 1623.

There followed, beside Walter of

Durham from England, the Roman masters Pietro Cavallini, Jacopo Turriti and Filippo Rusuti; from Siena, Duccio di Boninsegna, Pietro and Ambrogio Lorenzetti and Simone Martini; the florentine masters Cimabue and Giotto, with their assistants. In the XVI and XVII centuries there worked, generally on previously Painted walls, Dono Doni, Cesare Sermei, Giacomo Giorgetti, Girolamo Martelli and others.

As a result, no other Church contains such a wealth of "Bibliae pauperum" (painted cycles known as open public bibles or "Bibles of the Poor"). Never has so many famous painters over the span of 130 years collaborated in order to depict artistically, the earthly deeds and heavenly glory of a humble saint. *"Over the tomb of the Poverello, who died lying on the bare ground, there arose the most beautiful church of the XIII Century. Assisi became the "east" for Italian painting"* (Mario Salmi).

The stained-glass windows

The shrine of Assisi reaches its impressive climax with the suffused light of multicolored hues which streams through the stained-glass windows, unparalleled anywhere. *"Stained-glass windows are like Holy Scripture because they pour into the interior of the church the light of the true Sun, which enlightens the hearts of the faithful"*. Such is Pierre de Roissy's justification for the use of colored glass windows in churches.

Various groups of artisans from Germany, France and Italy all worked on the windows of the Basilica of St. Francis. Historians can still keenly trace the taste and touch of Flemish and English craftsmen. Begun in the middle of the XIII Century, besides the pre-eminence of antiquity among those Italians, the collection of stained-glass windows of Assisi boasts of a completeness of European national tastes and that of the unexcelled sketches prepared by Cimabue, Giotto and his pupils, Simione Martini, and other anonymous Italian artists working in the Basilica who have come to be known as the "Maestro di San Francesco".

The stained-glass windows are rich in biblical themes and episodes from the lives of saints, framed by a fascinating variety of flowers and plants.

The cultural significance

Having become a "man of another world" (Thomas of Celano) through his Christ-likeness, Francis had overflowed onto his contemporary world, a "new life," giving back liveliness to tired institutions and leavening others more caught up with the times. His way of thinking challenged outdated social and cultural processes and at the same time acted as a norm of a new era that would carry its enduring stamp into religious, social, literary, and artistic fields.

THE IMAGE OF THE "MINORE" CHRIST. Here, instead of the apocalyptic themes popular among the artists of the Middle Ages, we find depicted themes of the Nativity and the Passion of Christ. Thus Italian art drew inspiration from the book of the Gospels which quickly dominated the traditional scenes: the humble and suffering Christ came to replace the majestic and triumphant Divine Judge of humanity we find in the early Byzantine and Romanesque art. The Basilica of Assisi, dominated from the outset by its six huge Crucifixes and Crucifixion scenes, is essentially the church of a "poor and outcast God", not with the intention of reflecting the Saint, but rather his intense passion for the "minore" Christ. *"In the themes dealing with the passion, the sublime, victorious aspect was not emphasized. Rather, the accent was placed upon what appealed to the heart and the emotions. The immediate outcome of that impassioned contemplation was a heartfelt participation in the earthly sufferings of the Redeemer, a devotion to which St. Francis, both by word and example, gave a new impetus unkown before this time."* (G.F.Hegel)

Calling upon Christianity to return to a more evangelical way of life, Francis journeyed throughout the developing communes of Italy, proposing a more gospel-like and socially credible image of God than had been the custom in the constantinian feudal culture. "Through Mary," he used to say, "The Lord of Majesty became our brother" (Letter

to all the Faithful). In his great mission of reawakening Christian piety in the hearts of common people, Francis, who loved to call himself a "simple and unlearned man," could not have chosen a more appealing theme - one to which his hearers eagerly responded.

THE NEW ROLE OF "COMMUNES". Having taken upon

fact that, according to tradition, the church was the property of the Pope-Emperor, the murals ought to have been bright and durable mosaics. In this way the shrine faithfully portrays the saint who had renounced his opulent velvet clothes to put on poor wollen ones. The same theme in the mural paintings favor the image of "Lady Poverty", protagonist in the famous giottoesque al-

nothing I have ever seen more enchanting than my Valley of Spoleto!" For Francis, the material world became, once again, the sister of the spiritual world, as it was in the time of Eden.

This sense of fraternity with matter invaded the hearts and minds of the artists illustrating the Saint. Cimabue and Giotto would be the first Western artists to paint the characters of their stories in realistic places, with bodies that seem alive. Italian urban places and landscapes, particularly those of Rome and Assisi, become the stages holding the holy actors.

On the walls of the Basilica, the Sacred is not given the Byzantine glamour, but rather dressed in humanity. While it abandons the golden backgrounds symbolizing heaven, it dwells under the starry blue skies in the human city.

"God became flesh and dwelt among us." Proclaims the Gospel of John, the favorite evangelist of St. Francis. This became the main principal inspiring the new art. Faithful to this spirit of the Saint, Giotto recorded his legend in twenty-eight frescoes "where art was translated from Greek to Latin and brought into the modern way of painting." (Cennino Cennini). With these Franciscan frescoes, Giotto opened i Assisi, "the golden book of the rebirth of Italian art" (Adolfo Venturi).

himself the task of announcing openly the spiritual and material needs of the poor and the lowly, Francis was soon to find himself spreading the social idealism of the "communes". Thus it is fitting that the Basilica, built and decorated within social themes freely and joyfully embraced by him, should become the first center of "communal art." In the Upper church we find the first version of Italy's gothic architecture, austerely stripped of all redundant mural structures, as well as florid interior and exterior ornamentation that had characterized the northern gothic styles.

The Basilica's pictorial ornamentation is to be found exclusively in opaque plaster, despite the

legory in the Lower Church.

It must be remembered also, that Francis had enriched the vernacular language of the rising communes with the most famous of its earliest Pieces of literature: "The Canticle of the Creatures," the oldest copy of which is preserved in Codex 338 kept in the Sacro Convento.

THE REBIRTH OF ARTISTIC REALISM. Francis of Assisi had freed Christianity from the fear imposed by Manicheans and Spiritualists of avoiding the consideration of the human body as "brother" and the earth as "sister and mother." In a moment of rapture at the charming natural beauty of the Umbrian landscape he would even exclaim: "There is

"One can never stress enough, the importance that the Assisi artistic complesc has had for the European civilization. It became for Europe of the XIII and XIV centuries, what Athens and Byzantium had been for the Ancient world" (Federico Zeri).

Assisi art, budding from the franciscan ideal, signified the dawn of a new era, no less meaningfully than did the Saint whom it aimed to celebrate. Dante Alighieri imaged Francis as the "Sun," and invited all to no longer call Assisi the city that had given him birth, but rather the "Orient," having received from providence, the historical role of guiding cultural direction towards "new heavens and new earths".

The Lower Basilica

THE TWIN ENTRANCE OF THE LOWER BASILICA

Although small, the rose window with its richly sculptured motifs, has been described by Adolfo Venturi as *"the most beautiful church's eye in the world" (XIII Century)*.

The wooden door on the left, containing scenes from the lives of St. Francis and St. Clare, is the work of Nicolò Ugolinucci (1564), while the door on the right, the work of Pompeo Scurscione (1573), shows episodes from the lives of St. Anthony and St. Louis of Anjoù. The Renaissance style portal, crowned by a carving of the Annunciation, was built in 1407 by Francesco di Pietrasanta with the idea of providing protection for the doors.

In the small lunette between the wooden doors, we find the only mosaic representation of St. Francis in the building. It seems to be pointing out the rose window, symbol of Christ, "Sun of Justice" who reminds the pilgrim that, *"I am the gate. Anyone who enters through me will be safe: they will go freely in and out, and be sure to find pasture."* (John 10:9) For the people of this historical period, a shrine is like a door opened to the Kingdom of God.

The entry

In the entry of the Church can be seen the mausoleum of the **Cerchi Family** of Florence, surmounted by a decorative vase, the gift of the Queen of Cyprus to the Basilica. Another mausoleum (*shown in the photo*) is that of John of Brienne, King of Jerusalem in the XIV Century.

The central nave

The intention of the architect, Friar Elias, was that the Lower Basilica would serve as a crypt large enough to accomodate the throngs of pilgrims coming to honor the Saint buried in the center of the cross-vault. The heavy Romanesque architectural style creates a prayerful atmosphere inviting the pilgrims to pause before the altar of the tomb and open their hearts in intimate dialogue with the Saint.

The Chapel of Saint Catherine, Martyr

Chapel of the Crucifix

This gothic chapel was commissioned by the Spanish Cardinal, Egidio Albornoz, in 1367, and built by the architect Matteo Gattapone. The frescoes were the last of the original beautification of the Basilica, and done by Andrea of Bologna and Pace di Bartolo of Assisi in 1368 and 1369. The cycle relates eight stories from the life of St. Catherine. The chapel walls, outside the sanctuary, were frescoed in 1630 by Cesare Sermei and G. Martelli and depict the Suffering Messiah.
The chapel is dominated by a wooden image of the Crucified Christ, a magnificent German work from the XV Century. In this chapel a devotion is celebrated on the Fridays of Lent known as the "Corda Pia" ("Faithful Hearts"), an impressive prayer honoring both the sufferings of Jesus and the stigmata of Francis.

The Cross Vaults and The Walls

The Saint Illustrated and Celebrated as "Another Christ"

The vaults and walls of the Lower Basilica hold the oldest mural decorations of the whole Franciscan collection.

From the solid, massive pillars, ribs jut out, forming lofty frames for the segments of sky blue filled with stars made of tiny mirrors. These reflected the thousand oil-burning lamps flickering in the wrought-iron chandeliers.

(left wall)
SAINT FRANCIS
Francis divests himself of his inheritance
The dream of Innocent III
Francis preaching to the birds
Francis receiving the stigmata
Death and funeral of Francis

These frescoes were partially destroyed when the side chapels were constructed in the late 1200's and early 1300's. After recently being cleaned, the

Towards 1260, an anonymous artists known simply as "Maestro di San Francesco," decorated the walls of the nave with the two cycles of scenes from the Passion of Christ and the life of St. Francis. This was the first time that the eulogy "Francis, Another Christ" was affirmed and developed in art.

The similarities between St. Francis and Christ, depicted on the walls, appear in this way:

(right wall)
THE SUFFERING CHRIST
Christ stripped of his garments
Christ crucified
Christ taken down from the cross
Christ buried
The Risen Christ

Byzantine style appeares astonishingly fresh and life-like in the portrayal of the two cycles.

The Tomb of St. Francis

"Heart of the Shrine"

The stone sarcophagus containing the mortal remains of St. Francis is the heart of this sanctuary and one of the most popular places for spiritual pilgrims from all humanity. It was here that Francis of Assisi found his second and final resting place on May 25, 1230.

In the 1400's the tomb was made inaccessible and was opened for viewing only after 1824. With the authorization of Pope Pius VII, a team of physicians from Assisi and Perugia examined the remains of the Saint in 1818, and placed them in a bronze urn, gilded on the inside. Between January 24 and March 4, 1978, with the authorization of Pope Paul VI, a group of professors from Rome again re-examined the remains of Francis, and arranged them in a glass box which was then placed within the bronze urn.

In 1932, the remains of four of the first followers of Francis, Friars Leo, Rufino, Masseo, and Angelo, who lived and died in this place, were transfered from the Lower Church to the Crypt.

At the back of the crypt lie the remains of the pious and noble Roman woman, Jacopa dei Settesoli, whom the Saint referred to as "Friar Jacopa." She is said to have assisted at the death of St. Francis on October 4, 1226. She died thirteen years later.

A votive lamp, a gift of the Communes of Italy, burns night and day before the tomb. The supply of oil for the lamp is offered by a different region of Italy every year on the feast of St. Francis, October 4th. The lamp is a symbol of the people of Italy in continual prayer at the tomb of its most famous and beloved son.

Hail Holy Father, *way of righteousness*
light of the Homeland *norm of activity*
model of the minores *from this earthly exile*
mirror of all virtue *guide us to the heavenly kingdom.*
((Thomas of Capua, XIII Century)

Reflections of two Popes pilgrims to Assisi

"It may be asked: why God lavished on Assisi such enchanting surroundings, such a wealth of art, such a fascination for holiness which seems to hover in the air and which the pilgrim subconsciously senses? The answer is simple: so that we, through a common, universal language, might learn to know our Creator and to feel ourselves in solidarity with one another...

In the name of Christ our Lord and through Him, may peace be unto all people, unto all nations and all families; may this peace engender a much desired prosperity on both the spiritual and the material level which will bring joy, animating and encouraging all to strive for a more serene and noble way of living.

In the rock of the 'Hill of Paradise' rests the bones of St. Francis, the object of universal veneration. Francis had lived only forty-four years, nearly half of which had been devoted to the vain quest for happiness, as it is commonly understood. But some kind of restlessness tormented the son of Master Bernardone, and the other half of this life was devoted to a great and glorious adventure which appeared to be folly, though in reality, it was the beginning of a mission which led to everlasting glory. This mission and this glory provide the inspiration of our prayer here at Assisi, our prayer for Italy, for all nations...

O Holy City of Assisi, you are universally known for the sole reason that you are the birthplace of the Poverello, of your very saint, so seraphic in his ardent love. May you understand this privilege and bear public witness of fidelity to the Christian tradition which will be for you, as well as for others, the source of true and everlasting honor".

John XXIII - October 4, 1962

Help us, St. Francis of Assisi

Help us, St. Francis of Assisi, to bring Christ closer to the modern Church and to our modern world. You who have felt the needs of your fellow men and women in your heart, help us to be united with the Heart of our Redeemer. Help us to face the problems of our times, social, economic, and political. Help us to face the problems of contemporary culture and civilization and all the sufferings of modern humanity; our doubts, our denials, our tensions, our complexes, and our anxieties. Help us to understand all of these in the simple and fruitful language of the gospel and to resolve them so that Christ may become 'The Way, The Truth, and The Life' for the modern world.

This is what Pope John Paul II, the son of Poland, asks from you, holy son of Italy. He hopes and prays that you will not refuse him, but will help him. You have always been prompt to help those who have turned to you."

John Paul II - November 5, 1978

The Chapel of St. Martin of Tours

The **CHAPEL OF ST. MARTIN** of Tours is the most beautiful of all the chapels in the Basilica, not only because of its perfect gothic lines, but also because of its frescoes by Simone Martini and its stained-glass windows made from colored drawings by Martini.

In the arch over the entrance are portrayed Francis, Anthony, Louis, the king of France, Louis of Anjou, bishop, Clare of Assisi, Elizabeth of Hungry, Catherine the Martyr, and Mary Magdalene.

The cycle of frescoes show events in the life of St. Martin: his investiture as a knight; giving up his career of knighthood; giving his cloak to a poor man; his dream of Christ dressed in that cloak; Martin as a priest celebrating Mass, his being venerated by the emperor for the miracle of the fire; reviving a young person; Martin in meditation; his celebrating the funeral rites of St. Liborio; the giving over of his spirit to God in death.

On the back wall of the chapel is the donor, Cardinal Partino of Montefiore, greeting St. Martin, his protector.

The sublime frescoes, painted about 1317, are the work of Simone Martini, the painter of the Popes and Anjous, and demonstrate the influence of several factors. For example, one observes the courtly and courteous spirit that reveals the Byzantine and Sienese school in which he was trained, and the noble portrayal of aristocracy which is characteristic of this school; the theme of chivalry and priesthood which permeates the series of frescoes; as well as Martini's encounter at Assisi with the great art of Giotto from whom the artist inherited a more empirical use of space, lines animated more by gothic style, and a reality portrayed in fine detail.

The frescoes offer us evidence of the family and social life of Francis, who as a youth was brought up in the spirit of chivalry and wealth. The similarities of the two lives prompted Thomas of Celano, Francis's first biographer, to call him "a new Martin".

(at left)
St. Martin renounces knighthood as a way of life.

(at right)
The splendid portrait of Saint Clare by Simone Martini under the entrance arch of the chapel.

(below)
Detail of minstrels and singers during St. Martin's investiture as a knight.

The Chapel of St. Louis and St. Stephen

The House of Anjou honors Francis

Built at the beginning of the XIV Century to honor St. Louis IX, King of France, and Saint Louis of Anjou, a Franciscan Friar and bishop of Toulouse, this chapel was later dedicated also to St. Stephen, the first martyr, frescoes of whom decorate the walls of this chapel, and painted by Dono Doni of Assisi in 1574. They depict Stephen teaching in the Synagogue, being driven out of Jerusalem, and being stoned to death. The vaults of the ceiling contain prophets and sages: Daniel and the Eritrean sage; David and the Cumean sage; Jeremiah and the Tiburtin sage; Micah and the Persian sage. On the opposite wall are the allegories of Charity and Prudence, and on the arch of the entrance are those of Vigilance and Abundance done by G. Giorgetti in 1650.

Outstanding because of its gorgeous color and aristocratic effect is the stained-glass window executed by Giovanni Bonino from the colored sketches done by Simone Martini in 1317.

Detail of the window showing St. Louis in royal robes against a background of deep blue with lilies of the House of Anjou, kneeling in front of St. Francis who is blessing him. The coat of arms at the bottom is that of the patron, Cardinal Partino of Montefiore.

The Chapel of St. Anthony

Honoring the Wonder-Worker of Padua

At one time this chapel was under the patronage of the noble family of Lelli of Assisi and of the Dukes of Urbino. In 1610 it was redecorated with stories of St. Anthony by Cesare Sermei of Orvieto, assisted by G. Martelli of Assisi.

Outstanding for its artistic value is the pictorial stained-glass window with stories of St. Anthony, attributed to Giovanni Bonino, who executed them from giottoesque sketches. *"This stained-glass window represents the triumphant entry into the world of glaziery, a new way of depicting figures introduced by giottesque paintings, freed from insistant northern influences through the use of minute details and masterful care..."* (G. MARCHINI)
(below)
Detail of St. Anthony's sermon to the fish at Rimini: *"My dear brother fish, you are greatly bound, as much as possible, to give thanks to our Creator, who has given you so noble an element as your dwelling place, wherein you may have fresh water and salt according to your pleasure; He has given you many places of refuge to escape from the tempest.*
When, in the great flood, all other creatures died, God preserved you alone uninjured.
To you it was granted to preserve Jonah the prophet and after the third day to cast him up upon dry land safe and sound. You offered the tribute-money to Our Lord Jesus Christ, which He, by nature of His poverty, could not pay..." (LITTLE FLOWERS OF ST. FRANCIS, XL)

The Chapel of St. Mary Magdalene

The Chapel of St. Mary Magdalene was decorated around 1309 with stories of the repentant Saint taken from the Gospels and popular legends. The portrayal of body in the representations of the principal characters, the deep perspective of the scenes of both nature and architecture, and the poetic lyricism leaves little doubt that these frescoes were executed by Giotto and his skilled helpers.

In two small pictures, Friar Teobaldo Pontano is seen at the feet of the Saint, and Cardinal Pietro di Barro at the feet of St. Rufino, both asking intercession. These are splendid portraits of people known personally by Giotto.

On entering the chapel to the right, one can see some unfinished work. The interruption of this work, has left open the layers of plaster being prepared. The first layer of rough plaster, called "rinzaffo", covers the stone wall, the second layer, called "arricciato", is a smoother surface upon which the artist makes the rough sketch, or "synopia". The final layer, the "scialbo", receives the colors of the painting while it is still wet.

The Cross Vault and Transepts

St. Francis depicted as "Another Christ" and the "Angel of the Sixth Seal"

The superb decorations of the vaults at the head of the Church are the work of both the Florentine and the Sienese schools engaged in an artistic competition of color and theme. Giotto and his pupils on one side and Pietro Lorenzetti and Simone Martini on the other worked between 1310 and 1320.

The frescoes in the three sections organically depict and celebrate St. Francis in evangelical and apocalyptic representations. The four allegories above the main altar represent the Saint in the eschatological strife between good and evil: Francis appears victorious in the strife by affirming himself in Obedience, Poverty and Chastity in his own person and in his society. The framework of these "sails" depict apocalyptic themes dear to the heart of the Franciscan Spirituals. St. Francis in glory, enthroned under the "palio" of victory signed with the cross and the seven stars is a definite reference to "another angel rising from the East bearing in his body the seal of the living God" (Revelations 7).

However, the glorification of the Saint above the tomb, extends also to the arms of the transept, where the celebration of the holi-

ness of St. Francis is linked with representations of the gospel roots of that holiness. The story of the Passion, together with that of the Christ of Bethlehem, form the leit-motif of Francis, called "Another Christ." For Francis "*meditated continually on the words of Christ and studied his actions attentively; above all, he contemplated the humility of the Incarnation and the love expressed in the Passion of Christ;* these were so deeply impressed upon his mind that it was difficult for him to think of anything else*" (Thomas of Celano).

All Christian and Franciscan themes converged in what was to be a triple representation of Christ Crucified. Originally, an unfinished Crucifixion, the work of Puccio Capanna, was to be found in the apse, but was replaced in 1623 by a "Last Judgement", the work of Cesare Sermei of Orvieto. The two other Crucifixes are to be found on the walls of the transepts facing the choir stalls where the friars go for prayer and meditation. The Crucified Christ is fundamental to the spirituality of Francis, and touches the minds and hearts of both people and friars at prayer.

How he foretold that his body would be honored after his death

"*One day, while Blessed Francis was laying ill in the house of the Bishop of Assisi, a friar said to him with a smile, as though teasing: 'How much would you charge the Lord Bishop for all your sackcloth? One day many canopies and silken palls will cover this little body of yours which is now clothed in sackcloth'. For at that time he had a cowl patched with sacking, and a habit of sacking.*
And blessed Francis - speaking not with his own words, but with those of the Holy Spirit - replied with great fervor and joy of soul: 'What you say is true, for it will be to the praise and glory of my Lord'"

(Mirror of Perfection, 109)

The main altar, which is gothic in style, was consecrated by Pope Innocent IV in 1253.

On March 25, 1754, Pope Benedict XIV raised it to the dignity of a Papal Altar, thus bestowing upon it equal status with those of the Papal Basilicas in Rome.

The lavishness of the mosaic decorations on the altars, which the friars totally excluded from the walls of the Basilica, is a forceful reminder of the deep eucharistic devotion of St. Francis, who insisted that the Mystery of the Eucharistic Christ should be surrounded by the best that we had to offer. "*They should set the greatest value on chalices, corporals, and all the ornaments of the altar that are related to the Holy Sacrifice...*" (Letter to the Ministers of the Order)

The Four Allegories

The Iconographic Focalpoint of the Basilica

(At right)
Detail of "The Glorified Francis," vested in a deacon's dalmatic and coming from the sun. The absence of a beard represents the eternal youth of the Saint. It is the work of Giotto and his assistants.

(below)
On one of the beams of the cross vault is depicted the apocalyptic angel of the sixth seal (Revelations 7) to whom Francis was compared because of his stigmata and his role as prophet of Peace to the People of God. It is the work of Giotto and his assistants.

The main altar is crowned by the marvelous allegorical paintings of Giotto and his pupils (1310-1320). These allegories are inspired by the traditional and contemporary Christian moral literature centered on the theme of spiritual warfare.

The primary allegory sings of the glorious victory of Francis over evil in his sublime and brilliant enthronement. In the second allegory of **OBEDIENCE**, Francis is s.hown in his total openness to the Gospel and the the Church in his spiritual struggle against the pride and the moral anarchy of his contemporaries, both cleric and lay.

The third allegory is dedicated to **LADY POVERTY**. It makes use of the images of chivalry and of spiritual marriage in order to portray Francis' protest against the standards of the world, and his conversion and choice of lowly social status in solidarity with the poor, in imitation of the Christ of the Gospels. This is the "Manifesto" of Italy's common people since it is dedicated to the rising communes and at the same time, to the waning medieval feudal system.

The last allegory is that of **CHASTITY**. It is suggesting Francis' inner struggle against lust, the death of the soul, which prevents us from seeing God.

The Left Transept

With Francis on Golgotha

The cycle of frescoes on the Passion of Christ includes: the entry of Jesus into Jerusalem, the celebration of the Last Supper with the Apostles, washing the feet of the Apostles, the betrayal by Judas, the scourging, carrying the cross, crucifixion, deposition from the cross, burial, descent into limbo, the glorious Resurrection, and Judas hanging from a beam.

Opposite the grandiose crucifixion is the scene of Francis receiving the stigmata. The tryptich depicting Mary and the Baby Jesus between St. Francis and St. John the Apostle serves as the culmination of the entire cycle.

The poignant story of the Passion of Christ in the Gospel becomes integrated with that of Saint Francis. Pilgrims find themsleves simultaneously on Mount Calvary with Christ and on Mount La Verna with Francis.

These mysteries of the sufferings of Christ were dramatically captured in color and expression around 1325 by Pietro Lorenzetti. The fresco depicting the descent from the cross, shown below, marks the highest point of Gothic pathos, and remains unmatched in Italy.

Francis, the New Beloved of Christ

Lorenzetti's series of frescoes ends with the famous tryptich, the "Madonna Who Celebrates Francis," where we see Our Lady gently inviting the Christ child to bless Francis, who carries in his body a greater resemblance to the passion of the Crucified Christ, than the beloved apostle John.

This development of the comparison with the beloved evangelist as a comparison between Francis and Christ, was coined in Venice by a Cardinal Legate of the Pope. Rejected by two heretics, it was defended in this very Basilica by Pope Gregory IX, who, in 1234, had wanted to personally preside over the Feast of St. Francis.

It is only through the English Franciscan Chronicle of Thomas Eccleston, published in 1259 (conversation XV), that we have been able to acquire the thematic history of this fresco.

The Right Transept

With Francis at Bethlehem

The Nativity cycle, perhaps the most extensive ever depicted, includes the following: the Annunciation, the Visitation, the Birth of Jesus, the Presentation in the Temple, the Slaughter of the Innocents, the Adoration of the Magi, the Flight into Egypt, Jesus teaching in the Temple, and the Return to Nazareth. The three frescoes in the lower section represent two miracles of Francis involving young people in trouble.

Visitors, who carefully examine the vault of the right transept, find themselves drawn to contemplate with Francis, the mysteries of Bethlehem, developed by Giotto and his helpers beginning in 1310.

For Francis, whose piety reflected the emotional fervor of the common people, Christmas was the "Feast of all Feasts," and it is important to recall his contemplation and imitation of a living Crib on Christmas Eve at Greccio in 1223.

"Three years before he died, St. Francis decided to celebrate the memory of the birth of the Child Jesus at Greccio with the greatest possible solemnity. He asked and obtained the persmission of Pope Honorious III for the celebration, so that he would not be accused of being an inovator. He then had a crib prepared with hay and an ox and an ass...

The saint stood before the crib and his heart overflowed with tender compassion; he was bathed in tears, but overcome with joy.

The Mass was sung there and Francis, who was a deacon, sang the Gospel.

Then he preached to the people about the birth of the poor king, whom he called the Babe of Bethlehem in his tender love." (St. Bonaventure)

Cimabue

The **"Madonna** in **Majesty"** by Cimabue (1278-80), is one of the Florentine master's most splendid paintings. In 1310, the friars suggested a new iconographic plan for the vault and transepts to the Pupils of Giotto. The space actually occupied by the picture of Cimabue, as well as that covered by the two pictures above it, was to have been used for a larger painting of the Crucifixion, symmetrical with that of Lorenzetti in the opposite transept. A figure of Saint Anthony of Padua to the left was destroyed, but the rest of the Cimabue painting was saved from destruction.

The latest restoration of the picture has confirmed the various over-paintings and tamperings suffered by the frescoes during the last centuries, making it difficult to recognize any original work of the Tuscan Master.

Tradition has it that the most famous image of St. Francis left by Cimabue in this frescoe, is a reconstruction of the true likeness of the Saint which the artist developed from eyewitnesses. Among these were two nephews of St. Francis, Giovannetto and Piccardo, who were caretakers of the Basilica between 1253 and 1288.

The biography of one who knew him personally, describes him in this way: *"He was a most eloquent man, a man of cheerful countenance, of kindly aspect; he was immune to cowardice, free of insolence. He was of medium height, closer to shortness; his head was moderate in size and round, his face a bit long and prominent, his forehead smooth and low; his eyes were moderate in size, black and sound; his hair was black, his eyebrows straight, his nose symmetrical, thin and straight; his ears were upright, but small; his temples smooth. His speech was peaceable, fiery and sharp; his voice was strong, sweet, clear and sonorous. His teeth were set close together, even and white; his lips were small and thin; his beard black, but not bushy. His neck was slender, his shoulders straight, his arms short, his hands slender, his fingers long, his nails extended; his legs were thin, his feet small. His skin was delicate, his flesh very spare. He wore rough garments, he slept very humbly, he showed mildness to all, adapting himself usefully to the behavior of others. Holy among the holy, among sinners, he was one of them"*
(Thomas of Celano).

Two Polypitchs

Dedicated to Followers of Francis

**THE POLYPITCH
OF SIMONE MARTINI**

These five busts of saintly figures, painted in 1317, are another example of the dignified and aristocratic style of the Sienese painter, Simone Martini. We see protrayed, St. Francis, St. Louis of Anjou, St. Elizabeth of Hungry, and the married couple, Blessed Delphina and Elzear.

**THE POLYPITCH
OF PIETRO LORENZETTI**

The companions of St. Francis, Friars Bernard of Quintavalle, Sylvester of Assisi, William the English, Elect of Assisi, and Valentine of Terni, are represented in prayerful attitude above the place of their burial around 1320, which is protected by an iron grating. Near this painting is a standing figure of John of England.

The Chapel of St. Nicholas of Bari

The Orsini Family Honors St. Francis

The **chapel of St. Nicholas**, like the one facing it dedicated to St. John the Baptist, has been constructed in a gothic framework during the last decade of the twelve hundreds through the generosity of the noble Orsini family.

The anonymous giottoesque "Master of St. Nicholas," began the mural paintings in 1300 and scrupulously followed the Giotto style found in the Franciscan cycle of the Upper Church. The frescoes represent eight episodes from the life of St. Nicholas.

The finely sculptured tomb of the young Cardinal Giovanni Gaetano Orsini behind the altar is crowned by a fresco tryptich by the same painter. The stain-glass windows, in the giottoesque style, were realized in the first decade of the XIV Century.

The Chapel of St. Stanislaus

Of particular interest for those of northern Europe.

On the left of the nave, near the high altar, one will find a small chapel dedicated to Saint Stanislaus, bishop and martyr of Kracow, Poland. Because it was here in the basilica of Saint Francis that Stanislaus was officially declared a saint by Pope Innocent IV on 8 September 1253, that this tribuna, a balcony chapel was built to honour his memory. The sculptures and mosaics of the tribuna were executed by the artists of the Cosmati school about 1255. The incomplete frescoes of the coronation of the Madonna, and the martyrdom and miracles of Saint Stanislaus were completed about 1320.

Relics of the Saint

Giving Witness to a Way of Life

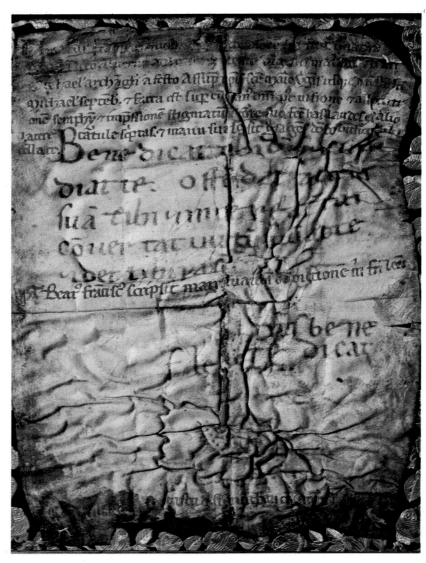

The **ASH-COLORED TUNIC** of St. Francis, expresses the lowly status and the humble way of life freely chosen by Pietro Bernardone's well-born son, who once aspired to the glories of knighthood.

After his conversion, Francis adopted the religious and social values of Christ. We read in the "Mirror of Perfection": *"Francis ordered his friars to patch his tunic with sack-cloth, and he always wore it as a sign and example of humility and sovereign poverty."*

The **CHARTULA** containing the hand-written Blessing of St. Francis to Brother Leo, who acted as his secretary, confessor, and nurse, is one of the most precious relics of the City of Assisi. The words written in black are by St. Francis, himself; those in red are by Brother Leo, who certified the authenticity of the document and its date of 1224.

Of all the relics reminiscent of St. Francis, the most outstanding is the parchment containing the **FRANCISCAN RULE**. Its spiritual and historical importance cannot be over-estimated. Composed by the "Founder of the Minores," it is introduced by the Papal Bull "Solet annuere" of Pope Honorious III given November 29, 1223. The parchment is justly considered the *"Magna Carta"* of the Franciscan movement.

"He used to tell his followers that the Rule was the book of life, the hope of salvation, the pledge of future glory, the heart of the Gospel, the way of the cross, the state of perfection, the key of Paradise, and the ratification of the eternal covenant. He wanted the rule to be understood and accepted by all... He also taught them that the rule should be always before their eyes, as a reminder of the life they should lead, and had bound themselves to follow. And, in addition, he wished and taught the friars that they should die with it before them. (Mirror of Perfection)

The Cloister of Sixtus IV

Rediscovering the Original Harmony

To complete the whole complex, which consisted of the Gregorian Palace, which also became a Papal fortress in the XIV Century, and the Sacro Convento, where the friars live, Pope Sixtus IV, formerly Friar Francesco della Rovere, built the great cloister in 1476, creating a harmonious gothic and renaissance architectural space behind the churches, characterized by grace and sobriety.

"Completely surrounded by the monastic complex - Chapter Hall, refectory, and dormitory - the cloister is the centre of this enclosed universe. It stands as an oasis, isolated from the evil outside world, and contrasting sharply with it. It is a spot where the air, the sun, the trees, the birds and the water of the well, recover the original purity that was theirs when a newly created world left the hands of God. The proportions of the inner courtyard suggest a perfection lost to a fallen earth: its four corners are co-ordinated with the four points of the compass and the four prime elements of creation.
The cloister, as revealed by its harmonious proportions, is part of the universe that has been preserved from the disorder that elsewhere afflicts the world. To those who choose to dwell there, the cloister speaks the complete and perfect language of the world of the supernatural." (George Duby)

The Upper Basilica

Italian art offers no greater example of the abundance of creative genius than that in the Upper Basilica of Assisi.

It is here the Northern gothic style of architecture, reformulated in the light of the Franciscan motto: "Poverty with Joy" (Admonitions of St. Francis, 27), found its first Italian expression, which is distinguished by the fullness of the wall structures, the elimination of flowering, influenced by Cistercian gothic, and the brightness of the frescoed walls.

The vast pictorial text provides the strongest evidence for Italy's transition from traditional Byzantine and Romanesque art forms to those of Gothic and Renaissance. This was realized by the last great representatives of the Roman school, Cavallini, Turriti and Rusuti, and at the same time, by the first Florentine and Sienese innovators, Cimabue and especially Giotto and his school.

Even the craftsmen brought from across the Alps to work on the stained-glass windows found fresh inspiration in the artistic climate of Italy. With the collaboration of Italian painters, with whom they opened up new horizons for glaziery, they created the exceptional complex of colorful windows.

"The Basilica of Assisi with its collection of 28 original windows, even if not totally preserved, forms a bright and fortunate exception for Italy, since it demonstrates with unique texts, almost exclusively by themselves, a half Century of Italian history in stained-glass work. Even with the depressing shortage of comparable artistic works that afflicts the peninsula today, one can see a liberation from the Northern influences taking place, beginning in the thirteen hundreds, and resulting in monumental paintings more typical of the locale. This new revolution seemed to spread as rapidly as that stimulated by the giottoesque art." (G. MARCHINI)

The Upper Basilica was completed at the end of the VIII Century and its artistic beauty, in wall and windows, echoes down the ages the greatest work of artists from all over Europe, and seems to proclaim:

"Praise Be To You, My Lord, For having given us Brother Francis!"

"Among the earliest and most important Italian versions of Gothic architecture, the central irreplacable element, is the Shrine of Saint Francis, set in the surrounding countryside of Assisi. The series of paintings which embellish the interior of the Basilica are in perfect harmony with its architecture, forming the supreme work of art of Italian civilization in the XIII and XIV centuries." (F. SANTI)

The Cross Vault and Transepts

The Great Work of Cenni di Pepi Known as Cimabue

To Assisi must go the credit of having contributed in a singular way to the artistic development of Cenni di Pepi, for it provided the Tuscan Master with space and opportunity to develope and express his artistic genius to the point of complete maturity.

The *four Evangelists* in the cross-vaults, the *Marian Scenes* from the Gospel in the upper and lower sections of the apse, scenes from the *Apocalypse* and the *Acts of the Apostles* in the left and right transepts, respectively, and the *Crucifixions* "for the friars" opposite the choir stalls (1277-1285) reveal Cimabue's genius for fusing old and new forms of artistic expression, more suited to the spirit of the time in which the Franciscan

message was working like leaven, transforming contemporary Italian society. The Crucifixion in the left transept, is an admirable example of tormented and tender compassion: Christ Crucified is potrayed in desperate agony, contorting his body with pain, in the midst of weeping angels coming down from heaven to join Mary Magdalene - the very climax of Cimabue's tragic pathos. Having received the idea from the crucifix picturing friar Elias, the one lost in 1623, Cimabue shows a sorrowful Francis at the feet of the cross in both crucifixions in these transepts.

The use of lead-white instead of lime-white in these mural paintings has resulted in their becom-

ing negatives of their original forms, through a process of oxidation.

"The Crucifixion of Assisi, compared with former compositions, shows us that the thematic iconography of the scene was broken by skillful hands - that the Byzantine crowds, all of a sudden, were animated with a new mood and movement - that the divine tragedy was renewed by Cimabue with iron energy. One still beholds the new miracle as if it were lightning in the darkness, and the miracle continues on the walls of the cross-vaults and of the apse.." (A. VENTURI)

52

The Wooden Choir Stalls

The Franciscan Community in Prayer

The choir is the work of Domenico Indovini of San Severino in the Marches. They were erected between 1491-1501.

Though not designed according to the traditional simple franciscan Gothic lines, these stalls are by themselves a most elegant and refined inlaid wood masterpiece. The sixty-eight different rosettes in the peaks emerge magnificently from the blue shells of pure classical Renaissance style. Besides the Annunciation, the panels portray the human figures of some of the first Franciscans, along with geometric and floral designs.

On the choral prayer of the friars

"I beseech the Minister General, my superior, to see that the Rule is observed, unchanged, by all, and that the clerics say the office devoutly, not concentrating on the melody of the chant, but being careful that their hearts are in harmony so that their words may be in harmony with their hearts and their hearts with God. Their aim should be to please God by purity of heart, not to soothe the ears of the congregation by their sweet singing." (St. FRANCIS, Letter to All Ministers)

S·ANTONIVS·DEPADVA·

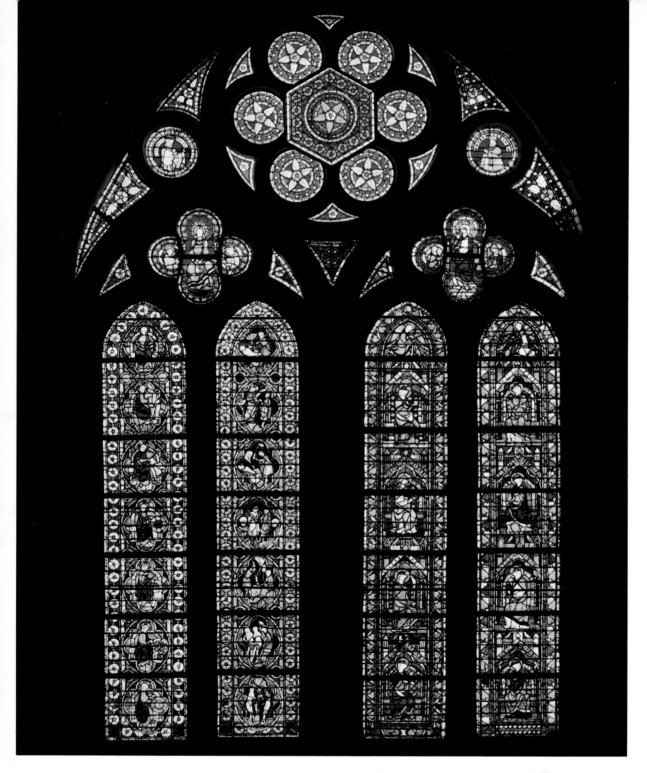

"The Basilica of St. Francis is not only a great franciscan architectural creation, corresponding to the activity of the Order and its monumental program, but also a model of the typical Italian gothic architecture in its use of walls, so favorable to fresco painting, its refusal to leave the walls blank, and its rejection of the building logic found in the Northern gothic." (L. GRODECKI)

In this example of Franciscan Gothic architecture, the structural lines provide a festive upsurge of this lyrical stone masterpiece of superb color and religious sentiment.

(above)
French stain-glass window in the left transept of the Upper Basilica, created in 1270.

The Central Nave

St. Francis Honored in the Concordance of the Two Testaments

Towards 1290, decoration work was begun in the single nave of the Upper Basilica.

The Friars, fully aware of the possibilities that these flat surfaces offered for vast iconographical programs, decided to portray several historical and theological aspects of the Saint's life. Francis is illustrated and celebrated in Old and New Testament typology, so that he appears as the personified "concordance" of the two Testaments.

Giotto's series of twenty-eight frescoes with the life of the Saint in the lower sections of the Church are supplemented by the series of biblical themes in the upper sections: on the right by stories of the Patriarchs taken from the Book of Genesis and on the left by scenes from the life of Christ. The three themes converge in the Center of the nave vault, where we see Christ blessing the faithful, John the Baptist, epitomising the Old Testament, the Blessed Mother, corresponding to the New Testament cycle, and Francis of Assisi, who is glorified as the perfect harmony of both Testaments.

The execution of this vast iconographic plan was entrusted to a group of artists of various schools and styles. The work of the Romans, Cavallini, Turriti, and Rusuti, can Be found along side of the work of the Tuscan school, new in its content and style: the Sienese, Duccio di Boninsegna, the Florentines, Cimabue, the early Giotto and others.

(At left)
Detail of Judas kissing the Lord, 1290, by Maestro della Cattura.

(At right)
The four Doctors of the Latin Church: Gregory, Augustine, Ambrose, and Jerome an early Giotto from 1292.

(below)
Isaac rejecting Esau, an early Giotto from 1292.

(below)
Painted drapery covering the walls below the life of St. Francis.

Giotto: The Life of St. Francis

This series of frescoes on the life of St. Francis elaborate three themes: St. Francis and God, St. Francis and Man, and St. Francis and Nature. Giotto's creativity is here given full and lively expression. The artistic and thematic elements make these the most celebrated and discussed cycle of paintings throughout Italy and the Western World. Trained under Cavallini and Cimabue, and Giotto's skill having been further developed by his contact with the sculptors of Pisa, Nicola and Giovanni, as well as Arnolfo di Cambio, this frescoe sequence can be considered the first mature fruit of the young lyrical genius. In these frescoes can be admired the striking use of space. His human figures are powerful and life-like, and their empirical backgrounds, whether they depict towns or landscapes, were a definite artistic development for his time. Giotto's St. Francis is shown in still recognizable Assisi, Rome, and other Italian cities. Thus Giotto's realism contributes greatly to make Francis permanently come alive for the pilgrim and tourist and gives a more graphic expression to the Gospel message of Salvation.

The twenty-eight episodes of the life of Francis, which Giotto and his school have depicted between the years of 1296-1300, were selected by the Friars who commissioned the work. They chose anecdotes from the "Major Life of St. Francis" by St. Bonaventure. Giotto's own captions under each fresco have been taken from this text.

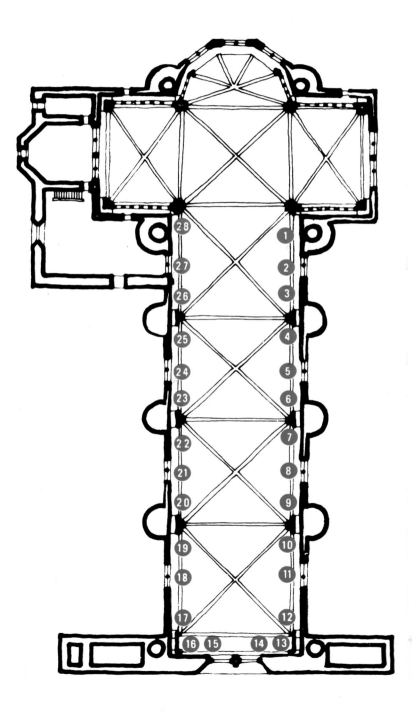

A citizen of Assisi spread his cloak on the ground before Francis who was still a youth. Thus he gave honor to Francis and asserted, under inspiration from God, that Francis was worthy of respect and reverence by all because he was going to accomplish great things.

When Francis happened to meet a nobleman, destitute and poorly dressed, he was moved by compassion and immediately took off his cloak and gave it to the man.

Francis saw in a dream, a splendid and sumptuous palace equipped with knightly armament, and with weapons embellished with the sign of the cross of Christ. When he asked to whom all this belonged, he received the reply from on high that it would all belong to him and his knights.

When Francis was praying one day before the image of the Crucified Savior, a voice from the image spoke to him and said, "Francis, go and repair my house, which is falling completely into ruin."

Francis gave back everything to his father, even the clothes he was wearing, renouncing his right of inheritance, and said to his father: "Henceforth with all certainty, I can say, Our Father who art in Heaven, because Peter Bernardone has rejected me."

In a dream, the Pope saw the Lateran Basilica about to collapse, but a little poor man, Francis of Assisi, put his shoulder to the building and prevented it form falling into complete ruin.

Pope Innocent III approved the Rule of Francis and gave the friars the mission to preach penance. To the friars, who had accompanied Francis, the Pope granted permission to wear the tonsure so that they might preach the divine word.

One day Francis was praying in a hovel in Assisi, and the Friars who were in Rivotorto, quite a distance away, saw Francis in a bright, fiery chariot moving around the place about midnight. The place was illuminted as bright as day, to the fear and amazement of the friars who were awake at the time, and of the others who were awakened to see this spectacle.

In a vision a friar saw many thrones in heaven, one among which was more glorious and resplendent than the others. He heard a voice say, "This throne belonged to one of the angels cast out of Paradise; now it is reserved for the humble Francis."

Seeing many evil spirits of social division and civil war above the city of Arezzo, Francis said to his companion, Father Sylvester: "Go, and in the name of God, cast out the demons... shouting at the gate." Sylvester prayed and the demons of division fled. Peace was immediately restored among those who were at odds with each other.

In testimony to the truth of faith in Christ, Francis challenged the priests of the Sultan of Egypt to walk through fire with him. None of them was willing to accept the challenge; they fled immediately from the presence of Francis and the Sultan.

One day when Francis was rapt in fervent prayer, the friars saw him raised above the ground with him arms extended heavenward. A bright cloud surrounded him.

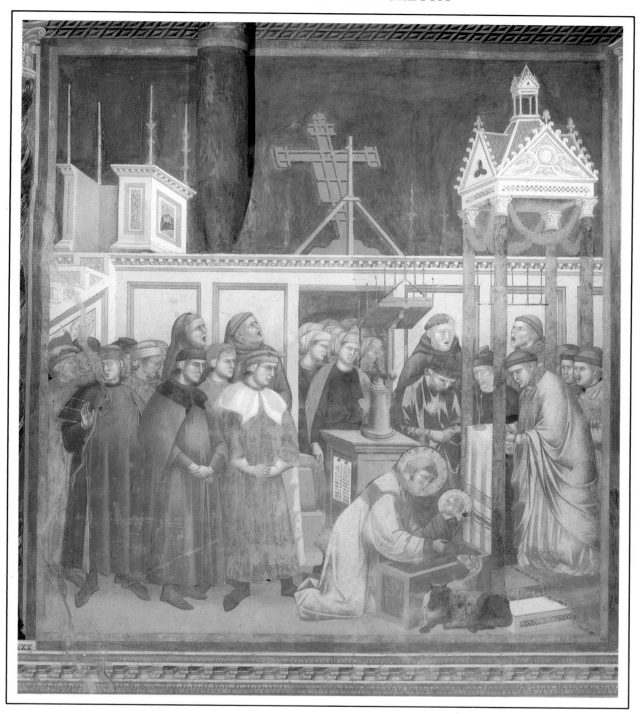

In memory of the birth of Christ at Bethlehem, Francis wanted to reproduce the scene. He asked that a crib be prepared, straw fetched, and an ox and ass be brought to the crib. He then gave a sermon about the birth of the poor King. While he was in prayer, a knight present for the ceremony, saw the Infant Jesus take the place of the baby Francis has placed in the crib.

Ascending a mountain on the back of a poor man's donkey, because he was ailing, Francis prayed and caused water to come forth from a rock in order to quench the thirst of this poor man.

Going to the town of Bevagna one day, Francis preached to a flock of birds which expressed their joy by flapping their wings, extending their heads forward, opening their beaks and even touching his tunic. The friars who were waiting by the roadside, witnessed this scene.

A nobleman of Celano invited Francis to dinner. Francis implored God for the grace of salvation for his host. The man made his confession, put his affairs in order, and while the others were at table the man suddenly died in the Lord.

Francis preached so devoutly and so efficaciously before the Pope and the Cardinals, that it was clear to all that he did not speak with the learned words of human wisdom, but with divine inspiration.

While St. Anthony of Padua was preaching about the cross at the Chapter of Arles, Francis appeared, extended his hands, and blessed the friars. A certain Monaldo saw this. The other friars greatly rejoiced.

Praying one day on the slope of Mount LaVerna, Francis saw
Christ in the form of a crucified Seraph which imprinted in his
hands and feet and right side, the sacred stigmata of our Lord
and Savior Jesus Christ.

At the moment of the death of Francis, a friar beheld the soul
of the saint ascending to heaven in the form of a brilliant star.

At the very moment that Francis died, Brother Augustine, Minister in Southern Italy, sick and near death, deprived of speech, suddenly cried out, "Wait for me Father Francis, I am coming with you!" Whereupon he died, and followed his Seraphic Father. The Bishop of Assisi, who was at the same time at Monte San Angelo in Southern Italy, saw the Blessed Francis, who said to him, "I am going to heaven."

While the mortal remains of St. Francis lay at the Portiuncola, Jerome, a famous doctor and scholar, touched the nail marks and examined the wounds in the hands, feet and side of the body of Francis.

The crowd which had assembled, carrying branches and lighted candles, transported the sacred body adorned with the stigmata, towards Assisi. At San Damiano, the procession halted so that Clare and her sisters might see the sacred remains.

Pope Gregory IX came personally to Assisi, and after the miracles had been duly examined, on the basis of the testimony of the friars, canonized Francis and enrolled him in the calendar of the Saints.

When Pope Gregory IX was somewhat in doubt about the wound in the side of Francis, the latter appeared to him in a dream and said, "Give me an empty vial." This he took and filled with blood that came from the wound in the his side.

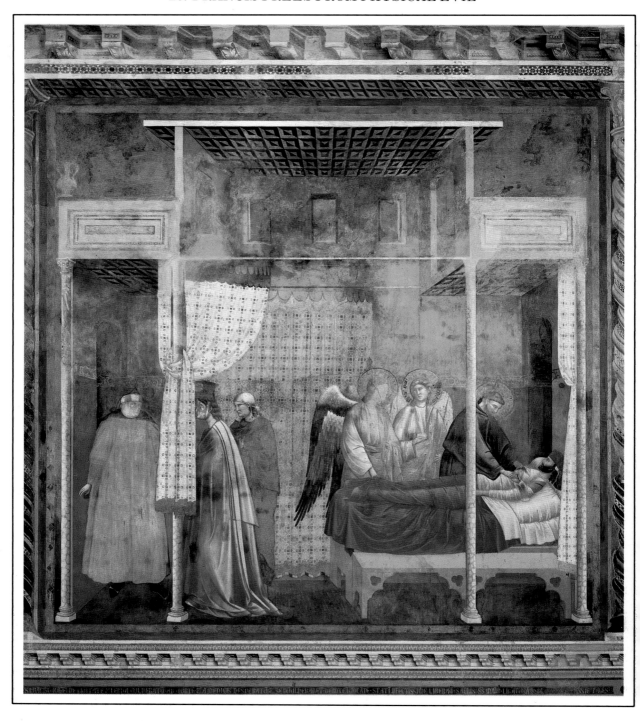

Francis undid the bandages and delicately touched the wounds of Giovanni de Ylerda, who was deathly ill, and for whom the physicians gave no hope. The sick man had prayed to Francis and received a miraculous cure.

St. Francis restored to life a deceased woman who had died with an unconfessed sin on her soul. In the presence of the clergy and others, she went to confession, and thereafter died peacefully in the Lord, to the confusion of the devil.

St. Francis liberated a prisoner accused of heresy, and by order of the Pope, had been placed under the authority of the Bishop of Tivoli. This happened on the feast of St. Francis. According to custom, the accused man had fasted on the vigil of the feast.

The Stained-Glass Window of "Maestro di S. Francesco"

The comparison of the spiritual childhood of St. Francis - "Unless you become as little children, you shall not enter the kingdom of heaven." - to the infancy of the Child Jesus, suggested this exceptional iconography to an anonymous glazier at the end of the XIII Century.

The saint, physically adult, is portrayed as a child in Christ's bosom, in perfect harmony with the same Infant Jesus held in his Mother's womb.

Rose windows laced the upper sections of Romanesque and Gothic Church facades. If the twin portals evoke the double nature of Christ (John 10), the Rose Window, sustained by the symbols of the Evangelists, recalls Christ as "Sun of Justice" (Matthew 17:2) and "Flower of Jesse" (Isaiah 11:1). In gothic times, the four symbols of the Evangelists offered further Christological meaning: the winged-man represents the "Word made Flesh," the calf, "Christ sacrificed," the lion, "Christ risen," and the eagle, "Christ ascending into heaven."

"The gothic edifice, with its transverse naves, represents the cross on which Christ died. The rose windows, with their diamond petals represent the Eternal Rose of which each redeemed soul is a petal." (H.A. Taine, *Journey Through Italy*)

The XIII Century portico of the Sacro Convento, built wholly from the white and rose colored stone of Mount Subasio, presents another view of incomparable beauty of the city of St. Francis. Perfectly Romanesque on the outside, the inside is a series of Gothic arches, invoking prayer and perfect harmony.

The Museum - Treasury of the Basilica

The "Gifts of the Magi" to "Another Christ"

The origin and the historical development of the collection of exhibits and art works commonly called the "Treasury of the Basilica of St. Francis," can only be traced in the light of eight centuries of local history.

The three sides of the Sacro Convento are evocative of much historical significance. The visitor approaching it from the direction of the Portiuncola sees the Gregorian Palace of Gregory IX, who laid the foundation stone of the Basilica in 1228. A person approaching from Perugia, sees the Papal Fortress, erected by Cardinal Egidio Albornoz after the "Constitutiones Aegidianae" of 1353-1367. The third side, seen only from the thick forest on the sloping banks of the Tescio River, reveals the humble, unpretentious dwelling of the friars, who still live there as guests of the Pope, and custodians of the Franciscan Sanctuary. Intended primarily as the Tomb of the most fascinating Saint of the XIII Century, the Basilica was destined to become the destination for multitudes of pilgrims and visitors, drawn not only from among the ordinary people, but also from among the aristocracy, both clerical and lay. These visitors, besides praying at the Saint's Tomb, often made generous gifts to the Basilica.

The Sacro Convento, enjoying the privilege of Pontifical status, was sacked and pillaged many times by the Ghibellines. But despite the sacriligious violations and damage of Muzio di Francesco at the beginning of the Avignon captivity of the Papacy in 1320, of Nicolò Piccinio in 1442, the Baglionis of Perugia in 1443, the thefts during the bitter feuds between the Nepis and the Fiumi of Assisi in 1420 and 1497, and the plundering and looting by Napleon's soldiers after the Treaty of Tolentino in 1797, the treasury of the Basilica can still boast of its pieces that confer upon the collection its unique and characteristic touch. Among the exhibits, the visitor will find paintings, sculpture, illuminated manuscripts, altar frontals, tapestries, and many other things, which taken together, can be regarded as "gifts of the Magi" to that "other Christ," St. Francis of Assisi.

A Flemish Tapestry donated by Pope Sixtus IV in 1479.

(above)
An oil **painting on wood** depicting St. Francis and four miracles that happened after his death, at the former tomb, and at the present one. The work is now attributed to an artist belonging to Cimabue's circle (1265- 1275).

(at left)
A splendid preliminary **frescoe synopia** design by a Roman Master taken from the representation of the Creator in the Upper Church (1288-1290).

(at right)
The crucifix is an exquisite and delicate piece of work by a pupil of Giunta Pisano, who was called the "Master of the Blue Crucifixes" (second half of the XIII Century).

(upper left)
The **Chalice of Pope Nicholas IV**. An admirable work of Guccio de Mannaia of Siena. Thirty-two miniatures in translucent enamel decorate the papal gift (1294).

(lower left)
The **Reliquary of St. Ursula** with an engraving on glass representing the Stigmata of St. Francis (XIV Century).

(below)
A fine Gothic French masterpiece of **Madonna and Child** in colored ivory (end of the XIII Century).

(upper right)
A **Cross of rock crystal** with lily-shaped ends and with applique decorations in gold-plated silver and translucent enamel (1330).

(lower right)
Altar frontal of Sixtus IV, designed by Antonio Pollaiolo (1472).

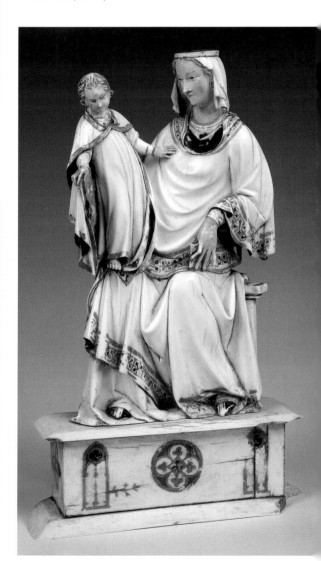

Why all these gifts for the "Poverello"?

"He who inspired the Wise Men, the Magi, to bring gifts and render homage to the beloved Child, His Son, in the days of his birth in poverty, inspired also, the noble lady, Jacopa of Settesoli, who lived far away, to come with gifts to venerate the glorious sacred body of His servant, Francis, who loved and imitated both in life and in death, the poverty of His Beloved Son."

(Legend of Perugia)

(lower left)
The missal of St. Louis of Anjou. A fine example of French art with Parisian Gothic characters and miniatures (1260-1264).

(lower right)
Crucifix and Saints Anthony, the Abbot, Francis and Clare of Assisi. Painted on wood by Tiberio of Assisi (1502-1506).

The Perkins Collection

The art critic, Frederick Mason Perkins (America, 1874-Assisi, 1955) was converted to Catholicism and baptized in Assisi, choosing the name of "Francis." For sentimental reasons, and in gratitude to Italy where he had lived for many years, he bequeathed his private art collection, in perpetuity, to the Sacro Convento, upon his death.

This collection comprises 57 pieces by the major and minor artists of the XIV - XVI Centuries, from the schools of Siena, Florence, Venice, Verona, and Emilia. Included are works by Pietro Lorenzetti, Taddeo di Bartolo, Masolino di Panicale, Lorenzo Monaco, Giovanni di Paolo, Sano di Pietro, Sebastiano Marinaredi, Sassetta, Pier Francesco Fiorentino, Barolomeo della Gatta, Signorelli, Fra Angelico, and many others.

Through this collection, Perkins made the echo of the Renaissance art of Florence reach Assisi, the city that had first seen the luminous dawn of that golden age of Italian art.

(below)
Triptych with Madonna and Child, Christ scourged at the Pillar, St. John the Baptist, by **Francesco di Gentile** (Fabriano, XV-XVI Century)

(opposite page)
Nativity of Christ with Mary, Joseph, St. Dominic and St. Catherine of Siena, by **Guidoccio Cozzarelli** (Siena, 1450-1516)

(bottom left)
Dead and risen Christ emerging from the Tomb by **Domenico Morone** (Verona School, 1442-1517)

(bottom right)
St. Bernardine of Siena, in a grey habit, the original color of the Franciscans, stands on a carpet dotted with tiny castles, by Giovanni di Paolo (Siena, 1399-1482)

(next page)
Masolino da Panicale (1383-1447)
Mary with child.

The City

The Setting for Francis and Clare

"May you be blessed by the Lord, O Holy City, faithful to God, because many souls will be saved through you, and many servants of the Most High will dwell within you, and from you many will be chosen for the Kingdom of Eternal Life."

(St. Francis of Assisi)

Surrounded by the medieval walls with eight gates; S. Francesco, S. Pietro, Sementone, Moiano, Nuova, Cappuccini, Perlici, and S. Giacomo, Assisi has many civic and religious places of historical, artistic, and cultural interest, located within its 424 square kilometers. Some of the most interesting are: the Pinacoteca and the Museum of the Roman Forum under the Piazza del Comune, the house of the Comacini, the Monte Frumentario and the Olivera fountain on the via S. Francesco, and the Marcella fountain on the via Fontebella. One also finds the oratories of San Giacomo Muro Rupto, S. Francescuccio, and Del Pellegrino with the XV Century frescoes of Mezzastris and Matteo da Gualdo. Finally, the Pro Civitate Christiana is a place of dialogue between the Christian faith and other newly emerging cultures, It includes a library, a gallery of contemporary Christian art and a publishing house.

The present fame enjoyed by the Umbrian city is due solely to the two Saints, Francis and Clare. For people today, the streets, squares, religious and civic buildings, are a spacious stage of the immortal human and Christian adventure of these two figures. Francis and Clare have remained the main characters in the history of the city which, with them and through them, will escape from what is the usual and ordinary, to become part of the extraordinary and eternal, like few other cities in the whole world.

The Civic Heart of the City

The present Piazza del Comune, stands on the ancient Roman Forum of which the still existing facade of the Temple to the goddess Minerva, from the I Century B.C., was the splendid summit.

From 1305 onwards, the Tower of the People has dominated the Piazza with its Ghibelline blackbirds, while at its side still stands the older Palace of the Captain of the People (1282). Facing these monuments, is the Palace of the Deputies, now the municipal offices, built in 1337.

The **Marcella fountain** on the via Fontebella (1556)

Kalendimaggio

The Middle Ages Revived Every Year

Each year, in Assisi, May 1 marks the official return of Spring. Originally, dating from the pre-Christian times, this festival of the "Calends of May" was only re-introduced in the XX Century with the hope of reviving the town's folklore and historical traditions.

People and city alike, divided into the "Upper" and the "Lower" town, commemorate old quarrels with parades in medieval costumes, cross-bowmen challengers, displays of flags, and singing contests along with the proclamation of the "Queen of Spring" and riotous feasting in the taverns.

This "Kalendimaggio" festival helps to reconstruct the medieval military and social milieu that marked the religious and social conversion of Francis.

The Church of St. Stephen, Martyr

The Bells that "Mourned" the Death of Francis

In the heart of a cluster of Roman medieval houses, stands the church dedicated to the first Christian martyr, St. Stephen. Its foundation dates back to 1166. The five spans, small narrow windows, and a tiny semi-circular apse, make an attractive, secluded, spot for personal prayer. On the left wall, there are frescoes dating back to 1400. According to legend, the bells of this church began tolling, on their own accord, upon the death of Francis.

The Cathedral of St. Rufino

The Mother Church of the City

In the V Century, A.D., Bishop Basilius built the first Oratory to house the relics of St. Rufino, martyred by being drowned in the Chiascio River in 238.

In the XI Century, Bishop Hugo incorporated the small chapel into a larger church, the classical remains of which can still be seen. The construction of the present Cathedral, designed by Giovanni da Gubbio, dates back to 1140. The decorations of the portals are of extraordinary iconographic interest, and an enigma to scholars, who are still trying to discover their exact theological interpretation.

The interior of the Cathedral was unfortunately transformed in 1571-1578, according to the design of Galeazzo Alessi from Perugia. It houses numerous works of art.

The Cathedral Museum contains illuminated choir manuals, silverware and paintings of great interest.

In the nave, on the right, is the Baptismal Font, orginally in the former Cathedral of St. Mary Major. It was here that both Francis and Clare were baptized. The Mother Church of the Diocese of Assisi, shares, together with the other Franciscan Shrines, the pride of possessing a precious Franciscan keepsake. In the sacristy is the cave where St. Francis used to retire for recollection and prayer.

"When at the beginning of my conversion, I withdrew from the world and from my father according to the flesh, the Lord put his words in the mouth of the Bishop of Assisi to give me counsel and courage in the service of Christ.

For that reason, and for many other eminent qualities that I perceive in prelates, I wish to love, venerate, and consider, not only Bishops, but even humble priests, as my lords."

(Legend of Perugia)

(below)
A detail from the decorations on the facade of the Cathedral: the lunette above the central portal.
(opposite page)
The wonderful harmony of the Romanesque facade and the bell tower, constructed upon a Roman cistern, which the visitor can still see today. The birthplace of St. Clare is on the left-hand side of the Piazza.

(at left)
Baptismal Font of St. Francis and St. Clare.

(above)
A **"Pieta"** in colored terra-cotta of German origin dating from the XIV Century, located in the chapel of the Madonna del Pianto, the original was stolen in 1987.

(below)
A **Roman sarcophagus** with mythological scene in which the Relics of St. Rufino were once preserved, located in the Crypt of Bishop Hugo's Church.

St. Francis Piccolino

"Born a Sun to the World" - Dante

The Oratory of St. Francis "Piccolino" was originally the cloth shop situated on the ground floor of the home of St. Francis. It was transformed into an oratory in the second half of the XIII Century by the Saint's nephew, Piccardo. In 1281, the exterior was ornamented by the addition of a large archway. Somewhere near the beginning of the XIV Century, an inscription was carved on the Gothic portal, which reads: "This Oratory, once a cattle-stall, was the birthplace of Francis, mirror of the world."

Inside can be seen the remains of frescoes dating from the end of the XIII Century, and others painted over them, from the XIV and XV centuries. Nearby is the Chiesa Nuova, built in 1615 on a Greek Cross, which encloses a medieval house, said to be the family home of the Saint, containing a "door of death", typical of many medieval houses. There one can see the place where Francis was imprisoned by his father, as well as the location of his father's cloth shop.

"By spiritually leaving his country, his kin and his father's house, Francis followed the example of our father Abraham, setting out for the land which the Lord had shown him by divine inspiration. So as to run all the swifter towards the prize of his heavenly calling, and to enter more easily through the narrow gate, he cast aside all earthly possessions, in conformity to Him who, though rich, became poor for our sake; with his riches distributed among the poor, his justice shall stand forever." (Gregory IX, Bull of Canonization, **"Mira Circa Nos,"** 1228)

Fragment of a XIII Century fresco.

External view of St. Francis "Piccolino".

The Basilica of St. Clare

The Memory Given to Clare of Favarone

Clare of Assisi, "the little plant of Blessed Francis" - as she loved to call herself - was born in 1194 and died on August 11, 1253. She was canonized by Alexander IV in 1255, and in 1257, work was begun on the construction of a Basilica in her honor. The present building includes the ancient small Oratory of St. George, once the tomb of St. Francis. In the modern crypt, built in Neo-gothic style in 1850, one can see the empty tomb, and the crystal urn containing the mortal remains of this Saint. In 1987, the remains were scientifically re-examined and returned to the urn.

The Basilica and the adjoining Oratory contain works of art from many schools.

The Crucifix of San Damiano

This famous XII Century crucifix of Roman-Umbrian style, which formerly hung in the Church of San Damiano, now hangs adjacent to the Blessed Sacrament Chapel of the Basilica. This chapel had originally formed part of the ancient Church of St. George, in which Francis had been instructed as a child, and where he preached his first sermon after his conversion. St. George's was also his temporary burial place, and the square in front, witnessed his canonization ceremony in 1228.

Precious to all lovers of St. Francis is this Crucifix which inspired his conversion in 1205. It is treasured by the city of Assisi as a precious artistic relic. Kneeling before it, Francis composed the following prayer which is considered to be among the oldest of his writings:

"All Highest, Glorious God,
cast your light into the darkness
of my heart.
Give me right faith,
firm hope,
perfect charity,
and profound humilty,
with wisdom and perception,
O Lord, so that I may do
what is truly your most holy will.
Amen.

SANCTA CLARA

Historical Tableau

(opposite page)

A painting on wood with St. Clare and eight episodes from her life by the "Maestro di S. Chiara" (1283).

The sequence proceeds from the bottom left:

1. The young Clare receives an olive branch from Bishop Guido in the Cathedral on Palm Sunday, 1211.
2. Having run away from home, accompanied by her nurse, Clare arrives at the Portiuncola, where Francis and his Friars receive her.
3. Clare is clothed in the Franciscan habit at the Portiuncola, establishing the foundation for the II Order of St. Francis.
4. Clinging to the altar, Clare implores her father to refrain from trying to take her back home by force.
5. Clare's sister, Agnes, resists her father, who refused to allow her to follow Clare's example.
6. The miracle of the loaves in the presence of Pope Gregory IX.
7. The final moments of St. Clare's life.
8. The death and funeral of St. Clare, celebrated by Pope Innocent IV in 1253.

The Interior of the Basilica

(below left)

The crucifix shows figures of Francis, Clare, and Donna Benedetta, the first successor of St. Clare, who had the work painted.

The Urn of the Saint

(below right)

"A lamp lit and burning so brightly could not be kept so well-shaded that it would not radiate its splendor and illuminate the house of God; this balm-filled vase, could not be so closely concealed that its fragrance would not pervade the House of the Lord..." (Alexander IV, Bull of Canonization, "Clara claris praeclara," 1255)

Fresco of the Nativity

(following page)

In the left transept of the Church can be found a XIV Century fresco of the crib scene. It is the work of an anonymous Umbrian painter under the influence of both the Sienese and giottoesque schools. It is a work of art emanating great sweetness and maternal love.

St. Mary Major and the Bishop's Residence

Here Francis Bade Farewell to His Former Life

This Romanesque church, originally the Cathedral of Assisi, was built over the ruins of a Roman Temple dedicated to Janus. Recent excavations under the medieval structure has uncovered a Roman villa which some identify as the house of the Latin poet from Assisi, Sextus Propertius (47-14 B.C.). The rose window of the facade bears the date 1162. Adjacent to the Church is the Vescovado, or Residence of the Bishop.

In the square in front of the church, Pietro di Bernardone, the father of Francis, publicly disinherited his son, and here, at another time, Francis, while very ill, brought about reconciliation be-

tween the Bishop, who offered him hospitality, and the Mayor of Assisi. On this occasion, St. Francis composed the verse of his "Canticle of the Creatures" which speaks of Pardon (1225).

"Praise be to Thee, my Lord,
for those who pardon one
another for love of Thee,
and endure sickness and tribulation.
Blessed are they who shall endure
these things in peace,
For they shall be crowned by Thee, O Most High.

(Legend of Perugia)

The Abbey Church of St. Peter

The Friendship Between Franciscans and Benedictines

The Benedictine Abbey Church of St. Peter was built between 1029 - 1268 in the Romanesque style with Gothic influences. The inside is large, with three aisles. The cupola over the elevated sanctuary is most interesting. Beautiful monuments in Gothic style line the walls.

Although St. Francis refused to adopt the monastic life-style and the spirituality of the Benedictine Order, firm ties of friendship and gratitude were forged between the Poverello and the monks of St. Benedict, who had been established in Assisi for centuries. It was from them that Francis obtained the use of his beloved Portiuncola Chapel in the plain below Assisi in 1210.

"Francis went to the monastery of St. Benedict on Mount Subasio and made the request of the Abbot that he had previously made to the Bishop and the Canons, from whom he had received negative answers. Moved by compassion, the Abbot consulted with his monks about the matter, and according to the will of the Lord, they granted Francis and his Friars, the Church of St. Mary of the Portiuncola, the poorest chapel they possessed.

(Legend of Perugia)

San Damiano

A New Way of Life for the Converted Francis
The First Dwelling of the Poor Clares
The Celebration of "Sister Mother Earth"

The setting of San Damiano gives witness to the first stirrings of the moral and religious, as well as social, conversion of the young son of Pietro Bernardone. Here Francis found the insight and the strength to take the first steps in his vocation of "conversion".

In a moment of intimate prayer, he heard an interior voice from the crucified God: "Francis, go and repair my house which is falling into ruins. "The Saint, faithfully obedient to this invitation, was destined to become the greatest reformer of the Christian Church. But San Damiano also gives witness to "most nobel poverty" through the "Damianites", the first Poor Clares. Together, the church, the small choir, the tiny garden, cloister, dormitory and refectory form the living space where the sisters, coming from every social strata, spent their lives dedicated to prayer and manual labor.

It was "near San Damiano" where St. Francis composed the greater part of his *Canticle of the Creatures*, and because of this, the place has gained literary as well as historical importance for giving birth to this *Umbrian praise* celebrated as it's first and most noble literary document, written in the "humble and withdrawn manner" of the people (1225).

How much the tomb of St. Francis became spiritually meaningful to every Franciscan since its beginning is emphasised by the fact that even St. Clare, on Christmas Eve of 1252, mysteriously "escaped" from the narrow and poor surrounding of San Damiano to refresh herself in the Sepulchre-Church of San Francisco.

"The Lady Clare said, that on that Christmas Night, being unable to get up from bed to go to the chapel, owing to serious illness, all the other sisters went regularly to pray matins, leaving her alone. Sighing in her loneliness, she prayed: 'O Lord God, behold I am left along with you in this place.' She then immediately began to hear the organ and responsories and all the office of the Friars in the Church of San Francesco, as if she were present on the spot." (Sister Philippa, St. Clare's canonization trial)

It was because of this vision that Pius XII declared St. Clare to be the "Patroness of Television."

The austere interiors of the Shrine of San Damiano: The Church, the dormitory where St. Clare died, the refectory, the choir, and the cloister.

The canticle of the creatures

Most High, all-powerful, good Lord,
    Yours are the praises, the glory, the honor,
    and all blessing.
To You alone, Most High, do they belong,
    and no man is worthy to mention Your Name.
Praised be You, my Lord, with all your creatures,
    especially Sir Brother Sun,
    Who is the day and through whom You give us light.
    And he is beautiful and radiant with great splendor;
    and bears a likeness of You, Most High One.
Praised be You, my Lord, through Sister Moon
    and the stars, in heaven You formed them
    clear and precious and beautiful.
Praised be You, my Lord, through Brother Wind,
    and through the air, cloudy and serene,
    and every kind of weather
    through which You give sustenance to Your creatures.
Praised be You, my Lord, through Sister Water,
    which is very useful and humble
    and precious and chaste.
Praised be You, my Lord, through Brother Fire,
    through whom You light the night
    and he is beautiful and playful and robust and strong.
Praised be You, my Lord,
    through our Sister Mother Earth,
    who sustains and governs us,
    and who produces varied fruits
    with colored flowers and herbs.
Praised be You, my Lord, through those who give pardon
    for Your Love
    and bear infirmity and tribulation.
    blessed are those who endure in peace
    for by You, Most High, they shall be crowned.
Praised be You, my Lord, through our Sister Bodily Death,
    from whom no living man can escape.
    Woe to those who die in mortal sin.
    Blessed are those whom death will find
    in Your most holy will,
    for the second death shall do them no harm.
Praise and bless my Lord and give Him thanks
    and serve Him
    with great humilty.

(top right)
Detail of Codex 338 containing the earliest edition of the "Canticle of the Creatures" (about 1253), kept in the library of the Sacro Convento.
(bottom right)
The tiny garden of St. Clare where St. Francis is said to have composed the "Canticle of the Creatures."

Rivotorto

The First Dwelling of the Fraternity Approved by the Church

"In the early days of the Order, when Francis began to have followers, he lived with them at Rivotorto."

(Legend of Perugia)

The present partially rebuilt hovels, enclosed within the neo-Gothic Church of 1854, recall the humble beginnings of the Franciscan Order, when Francis began to live the Gospel in fraternity and minority along with his first companions, Bernard, Peter, and Giles.

Here Francis wrote the first rule which was given only oral approval in 1209 or 1210. Here he trained his first sons in prayer and manual labor, and it was here, too, that in the spirit of prophecy, he foretold to Otto IV, who passed through the district, that his imperial glory would be short. Here he ws seen by the Friars as the "new Elijah" who was taken up into heaven in a fiery chariot.

After living for about three years at Rivotorto, Francis and his Friars were turned out of the huts by a peasant in 1211. They then took refuge at the Portiuncola. At the time when the first biographies of the Saint and the chronicles of the Order were being written, the Friars no longer lived at Rivotorto.

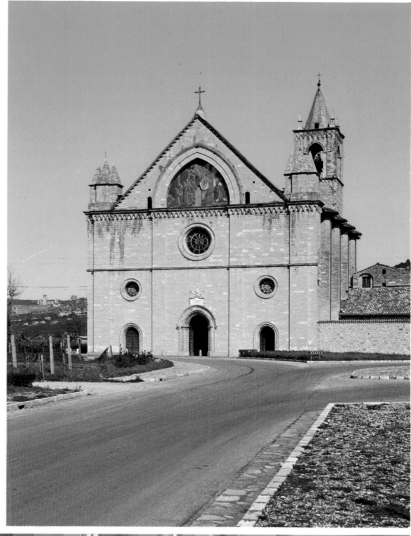

The Hermitage of the Carceri

The Search of Francis for the Infinite

This solitary spot called the "Carceri," had formerly belonged to the Benedictines of Mount Subasio. It was granted to Francis and his Friars as a place of retreat and prayer. In the XIV Century, St. Bernardine of Siena had a small friary built around the original XII Century chapel of the Madonna, preserving its simple rustic character. Here, the grotto of St. Francis can also be seen.

One of the Saint's biographers writes: *"St. Francis never failed to keep himself occupied doing good; like the angels Jacob saw on the ladder, he was always busy, either raising his heart to God in prayer, or descending to his neighbor. He had learned how to distribute the time in which he could gain merit wisely, devoting part of it to his neighbors, by doing good, and part to the restful ecstasy of contemplation. Accord-ing to the demands of time and circumstances, he would devote himself wholly to the salvation of his neighbor, but when he had finished, he would escape from the distracting crowds and go into solitude in search of peace. There he was free to attend exclusively to God and he would cleanse any stain he had contracted, while living in the midst of the world."* (St. Bonaventure, Major Life)

The grotto of St. Francis.

The small terrace and well.

Rocca Maggiore

Symbol of Waning Feudalism

This feudal fortress, the castle of Frederick Barbarossa (1174), crowning the hill on which the city is built, is an imposing symbol and reminder of the times of bitter civil strife. Its ruins recall the rivalry between Church and Empire, between the aristocracy and the common people, and between the cities of Assisi and Perugia.

In 1198, when the young Emperor Frederick II was living in the castle, the people of Assisi rebelled against their Teutonic overlords. They captured the castle, destroying its walls, seeking to acquire their civil rights. The present partial reconstruction was begun in 1367 under Cardinal E. Albornoz, as part of his extensive project of reconstruction throughout the Papal States.

Assisi at the time of the death of St. Francis, before the construction of the Basilica on the "Hill of Hell," by Franceso Providoni (1704).

Collis Inferni

Basilica of St. Mary of the Angels

Places Dear to the Heart of Francis

The present grandiose edifice on the green plain of Umbria, with its history stretching back one thousand years, is one of Christianity's most important spiritual centers. In addition, the Basilica of St. Mary of the Angels, contains a rich heritage of art work. The majestic Church, built according to the design of Galeazzo Alessi (1567-1679), with its modern facade added by Cesare Bazzani (1924-1930), protects the "Portiuncola," the church most loved by Francis.

"St. Francis was very happy that this place had been given to the Friars, especially because the church bore the name of the Mother of God, because it was so poor, and because it was called the "Portiuncola" or the "little portion". It had been forseen that it was to become the Mother Church of the Friars Minor. This name of "portiuncola" was derived from the plot of land on which the church was built, which was commonly known as the "little portion." (Legend of Perugia)

(opposite page)
The fresco depicting the granting of the "Great Pardon" on the tiny facade of the Portiuncola, a work by G.F. Overbeck in 1829.

The Portiuncola

This little rustic chapel dates back to the X Century. It was one of the three churches restored by the inexperienced hands of the young Francis, who, having taken literally the words addressed to him by the Crucified Christ: "Go and restore My house," began by restoring ruined churches.

In 1208, while attending Mass in this Chapel, Francis heard the Gospel passage where our Lord traced out for His disciples, His missionary style, enlightening for Francis, his own vocation within the Church. Thus, at the Portiuncola, Francis received from on high, the mandate of his ministry, to go forth and preach penance and the conversion of all humanity. So it was, that when Francis and his Friars has been turned out of Rivotorto, they established themselves in this place.

In 1212, Francis clothed Clare di Favarone in the habit of penance, giving life to the II Order.

But what has made the Portiuncola most famous, is the Indulgence associated with its name - the famous "Pardon of Assisi" which Francis obtained from Christ and which was confirmed by Pope Honorius III in 1216.

After the Chapter of Pentecost, 1217, which was held at the Portiuncola, the first missionary expeditions were organized with the Friars travelling to the countries of Europe beyond the Alps and the the near East. During the famous Chapter of Mats, held in 1221, which was presided over by the Poverello himself, Francis met the Friar who was to become his most famous son, known and loved all over the world, St. Anthony of Padua.

Toward the end of September, 1226, the dying Francis requested to be carried to the Portiuncola, that he might die there. Here, indeed, he died in the small infirmary of the humble convent, now the chapel of the Transitus. On the evening of Saturday, October 3, he gave up his soul to God, accompanied by the chirping of a flock of skylarks circling overhead.

"He loved this spot more than any other in the world. It was here that he began his religious life in a very small way; it was here that he made such extraordinary progress, and it was here that he came to a happy end. When he was dying, he commended this spot, above all others, to the Friars, because it was most dear to the Blessed Virgin. Before entering the Order, one of the Friars had a vision about the Portiuncola, He saw a hugh crowd of blind people kneeling in a circle around the church and looking up to heaven". (St. Bonaventure, Major Life)

(below)
The **altarpiece** of Hilary of Viterbo (1393), located inside the Portiuncola, represents the Annunciation and scenes from the life of St. Francis.

The Chapel of the Transitus

In the apse of the Basilica can be seen the cell where the Saint died singing, lying naked upon the bare ground.

From a simple infirmary, it was transformed into a chapel, and toward 1520, the interior was covered with frescoes by Giovanni of Spoleto, known as "Lo Spagna." In 1886, the exterior was decorated by Domenico Braschi. The glazed terracotta statue of St. Francis, that stands on the altar, is the work of Andrea della Robbia, in about 1490.

Gazing sorrowfully at the stigmatized body of the Saint, lying dead in this humble cell, Friar Elias, the vicar of St. Francis, was inspired to write the moving letter to all the Friars, announcing the death of the Founder of the Order.

"Before I begin to speak, a lament arises from my heart, and with good reason. My cry is like the roar of raging waters, for what I feared has come to pass, for me and for you; and what I dreaded has fallen upon us all, upon me, and also upon you. He, who was consolation, has departed far away from us. He, who carried us in his arms, as a shepherd carries his lambs, has departed for a distant land.

Since he was loved by God and by his fellow men, he has been conducted to the Heavenly dwellings in eternal light... While he was still alive, he had a meek and humble appearance, and there was no beauty in his face; nor did any strength remain in his limbs. His limbs were rigid through the contraction of his nerves, like those of a corpse. But after his death, his face became most beautiful, radiant with admirable brightness and most consoling to see. His limbs, previously rigid, became as supple and flexible as one could wish, like those of a tender child... Keep the memory of our father and brother Francis to the praise and glory of Him who made him great among men, and who glorified him among the angels. Pray for him, as he himself requested before he died, and have recourse to his intercession, that God may make us sharers, with him, in His holy grace. Amen. "

During the years of 1966-1969, the present crypt was constructed. The rediscovered rough paving stones, that formed part of the primitive convent, can be seen, as well as the outside of the "House of the Commune of Assisi."

In the shade of the Church of St. Mary of the Angels, the Order of Friars Minor grew, the result of the influence exerted by the Saint, on the people of his time. In 1368 the Observant movement began, resulting in a division of the Order, in 1517, into two branches: the Friars Minor Conventual, and the Friars Minor Observants. The family of Friars Minor Capuchin, emerged from the Observants in 1525. The First Order of St. Francis, composed of these three branches, continues the ministry of evangelization begun by him.

Beautiful enamelled terracotta altarpieces by Andrea della Robbia (about 1490) can be seen in the crypt, The altar (not shown) is the work of the sculptor, Francesco Prosperi of Assisi in 1970.

"Francis made nests for the turtledoves he had rescued from being sold. They began to lay eggs and to hatch forth their young in the presence of the Friars. So tame were they, and so familiar with the Friars, that they could have been domestic fowl, which had always been fed by them. Never did they depart, until St. Francis, with his blessing, gave them leave to do so."

(Fioretti)

Beyond the sacristy, with its spectacular baroque wooded cabinets, the work of the Friars themselves, around 1671, is the **Rose Garden** with its legendary flowers. One can also see the **Chapel of the Roses**, containing the frescoes of Tiberius of Assisi (1518), the **Grotto of St. Francis**, and the chapel of the Weeping St. Francis.

In the corridor leading to the courtyard of the roses, stands the touching statue of St. Francis with a nest of living doves in his hands.

The Museum of the Basilica

Among the many relics that record the long history of this Marian and Francisan Shrine are these:

(at left)
St. Francis attributed to the work of "Maestro di S. Francesco" (XIII Century).

(below)
The XIV Century **convent** with the small, poor cells of the Friars.

(at right)
The **Crucifix** of Giunta Pisano (about 1236). This is the most precious masterpiece housed in the Basilica.

Rocca Sant'Angelo

An Oasis of Prayer for Personal Reflection

Built on a hill, 11 kilometers from Assisi, Rocca Sant'Angelo is a rustic village that surprises the visitor, not only by its beautiful natural setting, but also by the wealth of art works that can be found there.

The Church, and the convent, with its XIII Century Franciscan cloister, can be seen in a prominent place. It is under the care of the Basilica of St. Francis in Assisi.

The small church has been adorned with many frescoes, the most notable among which, are those of Giotto's school, representing the Infancy of Christ. The series remains unfinished and can be seen in the small, XIV Century Gothic apse. On the side walls of the church can be seen a fragment of "St. Francis receiving the Stigmata," by Maestro di Figline, who may have been Giovanni Bonino of Assisi, "Maestà with Saints," by the "Maestro Es-

pressionista di S. Chiara," and other painting by pupils and imitators of the greatest Umbrian artists of the time, such as, Bartolomeo Caporali, Matteo da Gualdo, Dono Doni, and others. In the inset above the main altar, is a Madonna and Child between St. Francis and St. Anthony done by "Lo Spagna" in the XVI Century.

Another interesting artistic feature, is the frescoes painted by local amateur artists and commissioned by the devout confraternities of the village.

The Franciscan convent of Rocca Sant'Angelo was one of the favorite places of the Danish writer, Johannes Joergensen, who loved to return there to renew his ties of friendship with the simple country people of the district.

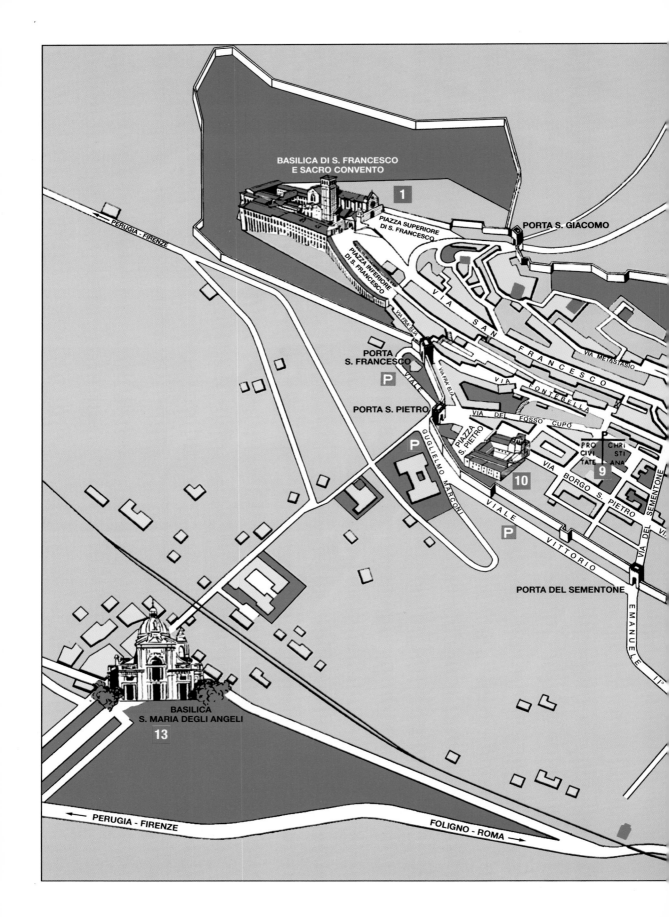

BASILICA DI S. FRANCESCO
E SACRO CONVENTO

1

PIAZZA SUPERIORE
DI S. FRANCESCO

PORTA S. GIACOMO

PIAZZA INFERIORE
DI S. FRANCESCO

VIA FRA ELIA

VIA SAN FRANCESCO

VIA METASTASIO

**PORTA
S. FRANCESCO**

P

VIALE

VIA FRA ELIA

VIA FONTEBELLA

PORTA S. PIETRO

VIA DEL FOSSO CUPO

PIAZZA
S. PIETRO

PRO CHRI
CIVI STI
TATE ANA

9

P

GUGLIELMO MARCONI

10

VIA BORGO S. PIETRO

VIA DEL SEMENTONE

VIALE VITTORIO

P

PORTA DEL SEMENTONE

EMANUELE II°

BASILICA
S. MARIA DEGLI ANGELI

13

← PERUGIA - FIRENZE

PERUGIA - FIRENZE

FOLIGNO - ROMA →

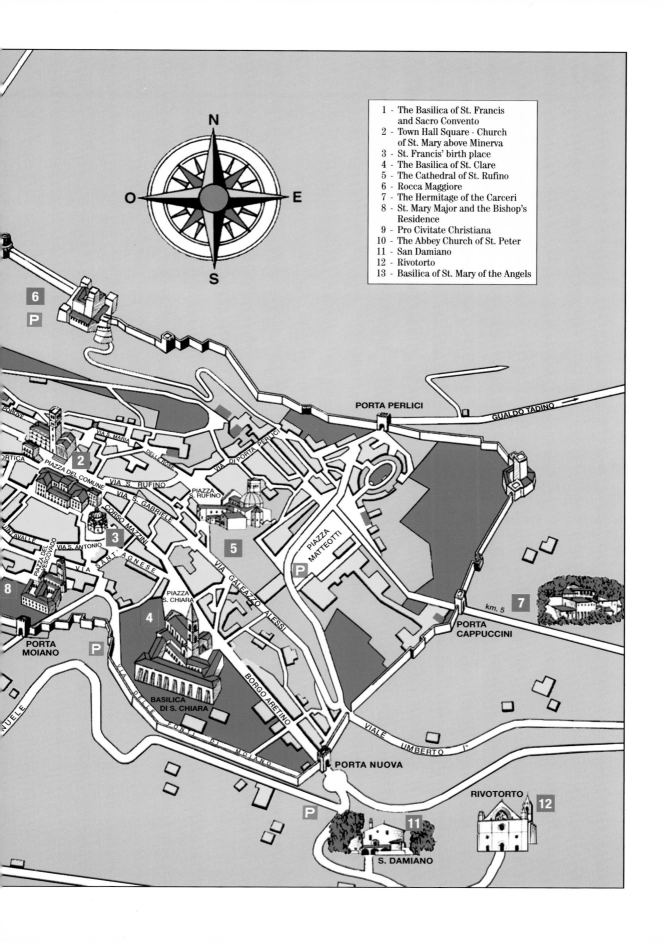

N

O E

S

1 - The Basilica of St. Francis
    and Sacro Convento
2 - Town Hall Square - Church
    of St. Mary above Minerva
3 - St. Francis' birth place
4 - The Basilica of St. Clare
5 - The Cathedral of St. Rufino
6 - Rocca Maggiore
7 - The Hermitage of the Carceri
8 - St. Mary Major and the Bishop's
    Residence
9 - Pro Civitate Christiana
10 - The Abbey Church of St. Peter
11 - San Damiano
12 - Rivotorto
13 - Basilica of St. Mary of the Angels

6
P

PORTA PERLICI

GUALDO TADINO

VIA S. MARIA
DELLE ROSE

PORTICA

2
PIAZZA DEL COMUNE
VIA S. RUFINO

VIA DI PORTA PERLICI

PIAZZA
S. RUFINO

VIA S. GABRIELE
CORSO MAZZINI

3
VIA S. ANTONIO

PIAZZA DEL
VESCOVADO

5

PIAZZA
MATTEOTTI

P

8

VIA SANT'AGNESE

VIA GALEAZZO ALESSI

PIAZZA
S. CHIARA

4

km. 5

7

PORTA
CAPPUCCINI

PORTA
MOIANO
P

VIA DELLE

BASILICA
DI S. CHIARA

BORGO ARETINO

FONTI DI MOIANO

NUELE

VIALE UMBERTO 1°

PORTA NUOVA

RIVOTORTO

12

P

11

S. DAMIANO

Table

Foto

Archivio fotografico Sacro Convento
Franco Cosimo Panini Editore S.p.A.
Archivio fotografico Convento S. Maria degli Angeli
Gerhard Ruf
Pino Antonelli
Marianna Noser
Fondazione Cariverona-Vicenza-Belluno-Ancona

Stampa

Umbriagraf - Terni